BRAIN

MY BODY

WRITTEN BY ANNETTE BAY PIMENTEL ILLUSTRATED BY TERESA ALBERINI

amicus
illustrated

Amicus Illustrated is published by Amicus
P.O. Box 1329, Mankato, MN 56002
www.amicuspublishing.us

Library of Congress Cataloging-in-Publication Data
Pimentel, Annette Bay.
 My brain / by Annette Bay Pimentel ; illustrated by
Teresa Alberini.
     pages cm. — (Inside my body)
 Summary: "Ava teaches her younger brother Noah
that the brain is like a computer, controlling the body
through the spinal cord and the nerves"— Provided by
publisher.
 Audience: K to grade 3.
 ISBN 978-1-60753-754-0 (library binding) —
ISBN 978-1-60753-853-0 (ebook)
1. Brain—Juvenile literature. I. Alberini, Teresa,
illustrator. II. Title.
QP376.P53 2016
612.8'2—dc23   2014037335

Editor: Rebecca Glaser
Designer: Kathleen Petelinsek

Printed in the United States of America at
Corporate Graphics in North Mankato, Minnesota.

10 9 8 7 6 5 4 3 2 1

ABOUT THE AUTHOR

Annette Bay Pimentel writes magazine
stories and articles as well as books for
children. Four of her children are all grown
up, but two of them are still working on it.
She lives with them and her husband in
Bluffton, Ohio. Visit her on the web at
www.annettebaypimentel.com.

ABOUT THE ILLUSTRATOR

Teresa Alberini has always loved painting
and drawing. She attended the Academy
of Fine Arts in Florence, Italy, and she now
lives and works as an illustrator in a small
town on the Italian coast. Visit her on the
web at www.teresaalberini.com.

"I wish I had a computer like yours, Ava."

"But you already have one, Noah!"

"I do? Where?"

"Inside your head, Noah. It's the computer that runs your body. Your brain!"

"That's not a real computer, Ava. It doesn't do anything."

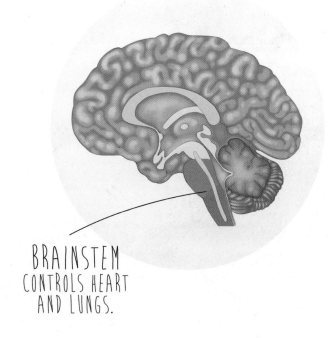

BRAINSTEM CONTROLS HEART AND LUNGS.

"Are you kidding? It keeps you alive! Even while you sleep, your brain makes sure your heart pumps and your lungs breathe."

"But I need a computer to play *Knights in Space*."

"No you don't, Noah. Your brain can think and imagine. You can invent a game with Sir Jim."

"Want to play knights with me, Ava?"

"Not now. But you can use my boxes to build a castle."

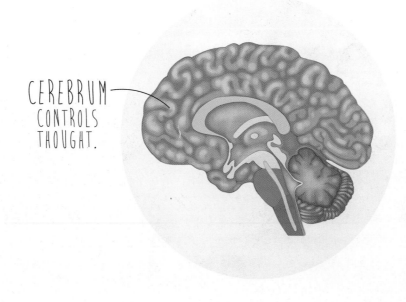

CEREBRUM
CONTROLS
THOUGHT.

"Look how many boxes I can hold!"

"Noah, be careful! Use your brain."

"But my muscles are lifting the boxes, Ava!"

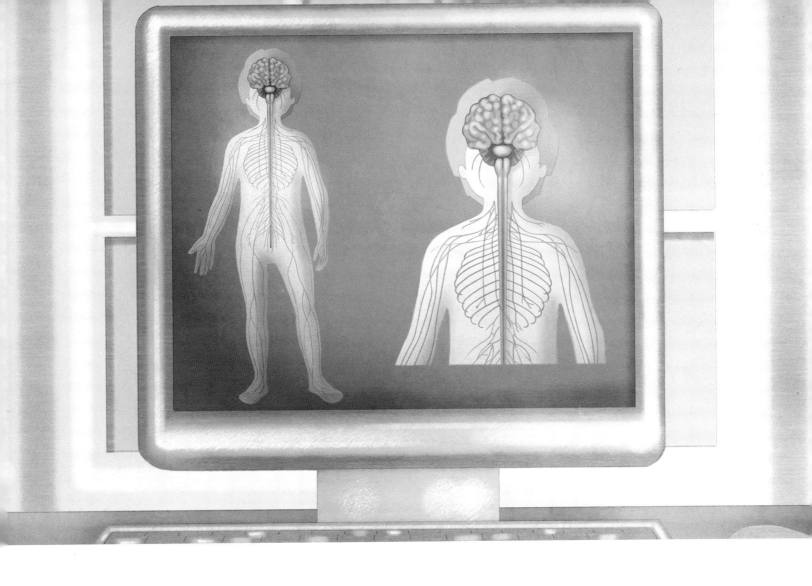

"But your brain's in charge. It connects to the spinal cord. Nerves connect to every part of your body. They're like wires to your brain."

"How do nerves work, Ava?"

"The brain sends messages along the nerves to tell your muscles to move. Your brain helps you balance, too."

"Watch this balance trick!"

"Stop, Noah! You might . . .

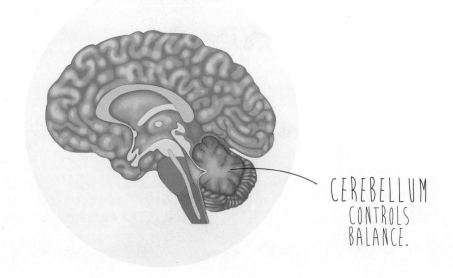

CEREBELLUM
CONTROLS
BALANCE.

. . . fall."

"Ouch!"

"Are you OK, Noah?"

"I fell. I guess my brain messed up."

13

"But your nerves worked great, Noah. They zipped a message up to your brain to tell it you got hurt."

"My nerves are fast!"

"Nerves can send messages almost instantly."

"Sir Jim's lucky, Ava. He doesn't have a brain or nerves so he never feels hurt."

"But Sir Jim can't taste these yummy cupcakes. You need a brain and nerves for your senses to work."

"I'm glad my sense of taste works!"

THE FIVE SENSES

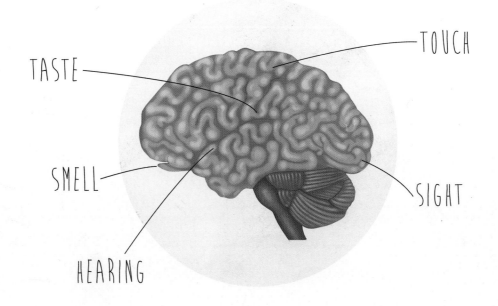

TASTE

TOUCH

SMELL

SIGHT

HEARING

"Your brain lets you learn new things, too, Noah.
Sir Jim can never learn he shouldn't stand on his
head on a chair."

"My brain learned that lesson!"

"And you'll remember it since your brain stores up your memories."

"Ava, how do you know so much about brains?"

"I looked it up on my new computer."

"You need a computer break!"

"Let's ride bikes. But wear your helmet. We want
to protect our brains!"

BODY BY THE NUMBERS

A **brain** weighs about 3 pounds (1.4 kg).

The **spinal cord** is about 17 inches (43 cm) long.

31 pairs of **spinal nerves** come off of the spinal cord. Smaller and smaller nerves branch off the spinal nerves—more than we have time to count!

Stretched out, the **nerves** in the body would be 45 miles (72 km) long.

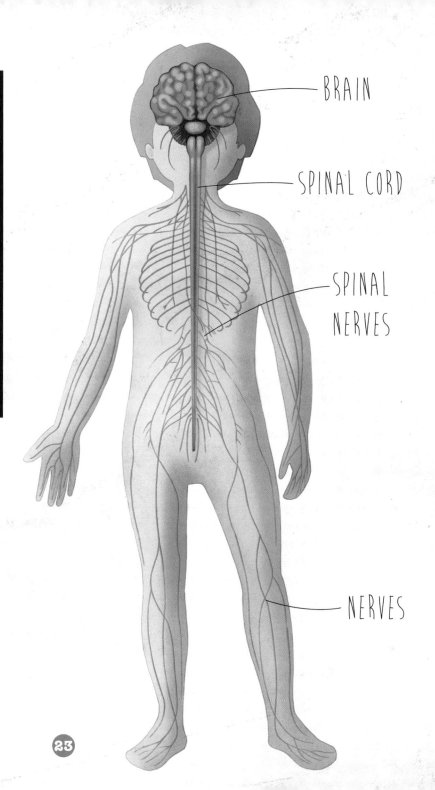

BRAIN

SPINAL CORD

SPINAL NERVES

NERVES

GLOSSARY

balance—The ability to stand or stay steady without falling.

brain—A body part that controls the other parts of your body.

learning—Getting to know something new.

muscle—A body part that moves in response to a message from the brain.

nerve—Fibers that carry messages from the brain to all parts of the body.

spinal cord—A body part that runs down your back and connects the nerves to your brain.

READ MORE

Ehrlich, Fred. *You Can't Use Your Brain if You're a Jellyfish*. Maplewood, NJ: Blue Apple Books, 2014.

Halvorson, Karin. *Inside the Brain*. Minneapolis: ABDO Pub. Co., 2013.

Kolpin, Molly. *A Tour of Your Nervous System*. North Mankato, Minn.: Capstone Press, 2013.

Stewart, Melissa. *How Does the Ear Hear? And Other Questions about the Five Senses*. New York: Sterling Children's Books, 2014.

WEBSITES

The Children's University of Manchester: The Brain and Senses
www.childrensuniversity.manchester.ac.uk/interactives/science/brainandsenses/
Animated pictures and diagrams help explain how the brain and senses work.

KidsHealth: Your Brain & Nervous System
kidshealth.org/kid/htbw/brain.html
View movies, do activities, and read more about how your brain works.

Neuroscience for Kids
faculty.washington.edu/chudler/nsdivide.html
A college professor shares fascinating facts about brains.

Every effort has been made to ensure that these websites are appropriate for children. However, because of the nature of the Internet, it is impossible to guarantee that these sites will remain active indefinitely or that their contents will not be altered.